Living Life at My Own Risk

Own Risk

The Afflictions of My Heart

Cynthia Powell

Living at My Own Risk / Cynthia Powell. -- 1st ed.
ISBN 978-0-692-56284-0

Cynthia Powell can be contacted for speaking engagements through Facebook or twitter @cynthiapowell.

Books may be ordered through booksellers or by contacting Cynthia Powell directly.

Dedication

I would like to dedicate LIVING LIFE AT MY OWN RISK to my mom, dad, my two beautiful girls Tiffini and Tamyka, my sister, my niece, my nephews, my son in law and my wonderful grandchildren. I have learned so much from each and every one of you. Thank you for all of your love and support.

To my real friends who were there for me and loved me unconditionally, you know who you are, I truly thank you!

I especially want to dedicate this book to those who don't have a voice. I hope this book brings some healing to your soul and will help you find some peace in this world.

I would further like to send a special thank you and love to R.G. Shelton, Pastor Gloria Boyce, Zoeland Writer's Club and Robert Covington.

Lastly, I am thankful for the chosen gift of happiness.

CONTENTS

CHAPTER 1 Innocent and Naïve   1

CHAPTER 2 What Was I Thinking?   7

CHAPTER 3 Journey Like No Other   15

CHAPTER 4 Faith of A Mustard Seed   19

CHAPTER 5 Didn't See This Coming   25

CHAPTER 6 The Fallout   29

CHAPTER 7 Living with My Demons   31

CHAPTER 8 End of My Rope   35

CHAPTER 9 Starting Over   39

FOREWORD

LIVING LIFE AT MY OWN RISK is a story of a young girl's innocence being taken from her causing her to have to adapt and grow up faster than desired or expected. The author uses her life experiences to shed light on common issues of young women and men. Exposing the dark side of bullying, violence and sexual abuse.

The book begins with the author entering high school at the age of fourteen. Already an awkward young girl trying to grow into her body, the author deals with being overweight and at an increased risk of being the target for bullies. Body image issues usually impact the self-esteem. This is found to be true for the author. The low self-esteem the author experienced caused her to become caught in a vicious cycle of self-destructive behavior. Further complicating her ability to feel adequate, lovable or competent. The constant bullying and the author's own doubts of self created faulty assumptions and self-defeating behaviors.

The culmination of the things the author experienced prevented her from moving forward in the direction she desired for her own life. Often compromising for love and acceptance. To the point she became routinely abused. This is modern day book addressing today's real life issues. It is a must read for all young people entering adulthood and a mirror for all who are caught in the vicious cycle of mental, emotional, sexual, verbal or physical abuse of any and all kinds as well as the bullies, betrayers of confidence and perpetrators. Receive the message to be a safe place of confidence and uplift. Don't continue to abuse someone who has or is abused.

CHAPTER ONE

Innocent and Naïve

You never know what life has in store for you. All you can do is make it the best way you can. This is where my journey begins. My first day of school what could be more awkward. I was starting my first day of junior high while trying to come into my own. That can be so hard. You're meeting new kids for the first time, and they come from all different walks of life. For sure, you could see kids were raised differently. I don't think you realize how sheltered you have been from some things until you attend school with other kids.

Trying to Fit In

Besides all of that, I was a little nervous and uneasy, not sure of what the other kids would think of me. I was a plus- sized young lady and still not comfortable in my own skin. Being on the husky side wasn't in for sure. The kids were so cruel. They used the word *fat*, plain and simple. Some kids have no idea when they tease and say things to you that you carry some of those things your whole lifetime.

You hopefully, at some point, you do make a few good friends who like you for you. I tried to get myself interested in things in school, like science club and working on the school newspaper. Not the typical things like drama and cheerleading. I had to get in where I could fit in. Just taking a chance trying out for track, I found out I could throw the hell out of a shot putt. I could also play volley ball pretty well also.

Boy Crazy

I was slowly feeling my way, I suppose. If that wasn't complicated enough, I also started noticing boys, of course, like any other young girl with raging hormones that she seems to have no control over. They weren't noticing me much though. I didn't fit the typical body type. They only noticed the cheerleaders and the skinny girls.

That didn't stop me from having my eyes on a few boys anyway. It really wasn't me; it was my uncontrollable teenage hormones. One day, I spotted this young man in the hall. I found out his name was Leonardo. I thought he was handsome. I loved his voice. It was different. It sounded like it could have been a radio voice. His name wasn't a common one you heard all the time. I noticed him, but of course he didn't notice me right away at the beginning. I had a crush on him for sure. He hadn't been at school too long, and he had a girlfriend already. I wasn't surprised. I just tried to keep my distance. I liked him from a far. LOL!!

We just passed each other in the hallway every day. He would speak to me at some after- school functions. We would have conversations sometimes. It truly was a one- sided crush on my part. He had a girlfriend. It went on like this for the rest of the school year. We were just like two ships passing in the night. Before I knew it, the school year's end was fast approaching and summer vacation was upon us. Though the summer months seemed to go by quickly, it felt longer because I wasn't able to talk to him or see him during this time. The months couldn't go by fast enough for me! I couldn't wait for school to start again. I had no idea how to deal with my clueless fourteen- year- old feelings.

New School Year Begins

The next year rolled around, and school was back in. It caught me off guard because we ended up having a class together. Go figure. I started trying to talk to him a little bit. He would talk about some of the classes he was in, and we had a little general conversation. In my mind, it was a start anyway. I know by now you are thinking all I did was talk about Leonardo when I was supposed to be in school to learn. I did do pretty well in school, and I was in the orchestra too! I was at that age though where I was noticing boys. My mind was on him as well as my studies. I thought that at least he was talking to me at some point. I would see Leonardo in the hall sometimes and smile at him. He would smile back. He would wink at me, and I would wink back. I thought from his response that he was somewhat interested.

I would talk to him every now and then. He would ask me how I was doing and how my day was going, little things like that. He just always seemed to be so pleasant. At this point, I decided to ask him if we could exchange phone numbers and talk sometime.

He did take my number, but he didn't give me his. He said he would call me sometime. I guess I didn't let it phase me that he took my number and didn't give me his. In my mind, I figured if he really did call, he was actually interested. I think about two weeks or so went by and he did call me. We talked about the things we had in common with each other, our likes and dislikes. It seemed that we were getting closer as time went on.

I would say about eight more weeks went by, and we were talking on a regular basis. He considered me a friend. I liked him, though but at this time, the relationship was on a friendship basis. Sometimes we would have some intense conversations as intense as you could at fourteen. I was not sure where that was going yet on his part. Although he did mention to me that he cared about me. I still wasn't sure if he had started developing feelings for me.

He shocked me one day. Out of the blue he asked me if I would go out with him. I asked him what his current girlfriend would say about that. He told me they had broken up. Maybe I should have asked him what happened, but I didn't. I liked him so much that I hoped he wanted to date me. So what does he do? He asked me if we could go out sometime.

I said yes! I had no idea what I was saying yes too really. For heaven's sake, I was so young.' We started going out on dates. At our age, going out on a date was doing homework in the library or hanging out at school functions. I was too young to be on a date anyway. My parents weren't having that. That darn puberty was something else. Here is a definition of puberty: the stage of human physical development in which sexual reproduction can first occur. This definition does not encompass half of the emotional, physical, and mental changes your body goes through. I had no clue.

It seemed to be going okay though. The problem was I had nothing to base it on at my age. In all young relationships, you have some disagreements. We were no exception! This is especially true when you try to do adult things when you're not one. You are not even ready for that yet. I didn't ask my parents if it was okay. I just took it upon myself. I know they wouldn't have agreed. That's probably why I should not have done it. The fact that I was doing it without them being aware of it should have been my first indication it was not right. I was hardheaded and did it anyway.

Ignoring the Signs

It really was still a learning- as- you- go process. We both were still trying to learn about our own bodies and emotions. What really touched me at this time was he seemed to like me for me. That was important to me. The way he held my hand and the way he looked at me. I felt like he was really sincere.

We would have some small arguments. He would get upset pretty quickly. That would worry me a little sometimes. How someone that young could get upset like that. I guess maybe sometimes we overlook some things because you really don't know what people are going through at home sometimes. I had experienced some things in my young life that I never told anybody about. I guess that's why I tried to understand. I guess I would ignore it because he would apologize for losing his temper. "He said", he would work on it. Some months went by, and it was going all right. He would have and outburst every now and then. I was still getting to know him.

I guess I was what you would call a hopeless romantic even though I was not mature enough to totally understand that yet either. I truly believed in unconditional love. I also had to come to accept the reality that everything wasn't teddy bears and roses. Lol! I realized you have to work at relationships. I had to understand you we're going to have good days as well as some bad. Starting out a young women, I would beat up on the boys because of the crazy stories I would hear, like "Be careful; they only want to sleep with you to get notches on their belt." I figured the longer I beat up on them, the better off I'd be.

Not only that, my friends and I would hang out and the older boys would try to come at us. The things they would say to us of a sexual nature were way too much. I really stayed away from them. They were truly out of my league and I knew it. I was okay with not being on that level. Sex seemed to be the only thing on their minds. I had to remember that as a young person, sometimes when we are away from our parents we do some strange things. These things we know we weren't brought up to do. Why is it you have to learn a lesson yourself the hard way first before you totally understand it? It would be so much better to humble ourselves and listen.

CHAPTER TWO

What Was I Thinking?

As the school year came to a close my virginity was still intact and I was trying hard to keep it that way. Boys will be boys, so they are going to try. Leonardo was trying to wear me down by telling me he loved me. Even though we were both young and our hormones had no clue what sex meant or what it entailed, it was an ever present discussion. He was starting to wear me down. I tried to put him off as long as I could.

OMG!!! In my heart, I felt like I was not ready for sex, but those crazy all- over- the- place hormones took over. I gave in against my better judgment. If I knew then what I now know, I would have waited until I was more mature. Although I gave, in, my pain from the way I felt about myself at that time ran much deeper than I realized. I wasn't ready physically or mentally for this to happen.

It hurt something awful. It was fast, and I had no clue what I was doing at that moment. I promise you I never wanted to do it again after what I went through. I was only fourteen. My body may have looked older than that, but I wasn't ready at all. I was so damn smart and mature for my age I didn't even know I was pregnant. It happened so fast. I didn't even think you could get pregnant your first time.

I just thought I had come down with the flu. I missed a period. That should have been my sign, but I just thought it was a little late so I didn't worry much about it. I was so young, what did I really know? I was nauseated, throwing up and having pain in my stomach. I told my mom how I was feeling. She made a doctor's appointment. I still didn't have a clue as to what was going on with me.

I got to the doctor's office to have my first adult vaginal exam. The doctor inserted his finger into my vagina to check me. I felt so violated and ashamed. The doctor then asked me to sit up. He confirmed that I was pregnant. *Oh my goodness!* I was so out done when I realized it. I thought my mom would be more upset than I was. It was a good thing she wasn't. I could not have handled anything more. Someone had to keep a level head because I felt out of my body at this point. It was the worst feeling!

Disappointed in Myself

I felt like I had let my parents down. I think the reason I let it happen at that time was because I was looking for love, acceptance, and approval, just to name a few. I realized at that point that wasn't the way to get it. I truly didn't know or understand my worth.

I thought I knew it all. "NOT"! The news shocked me into reality. I thought to myself, "this baby is going to make me or break me". Either way, I had to make a choice. I had to decide to keep or terminate this life growing inside of me. I chose to take on my responsibility and try to be as mature as I could be for my age. After my doctor's appointment, I had to go back to school and act like nothing was wrong. I walked around in school that day in a daze. I just couldn't believe I was really pregnant! During my time in school, it was frowned upon to be pregnant at a young age. I had to keep it a secret. I was able to hide it pretty well. I was a healthy young lady, and I wore a coat most of the time during my pregnancy.

I was fortunate I didn't have much morning sickness or any issues until the end of my pregnancy. I hung in there until it was time to give birth. I had to leave school so no one would know the reason why I wasn't in school. I used the reason that my blood pressure was elevated so I had to be off until I got it under control. I was off a few weeks, and nosey kids were calling. They said they wanted to see how I was doing, but they really did not. They were just trying to get in my business. I told only a couple of my supposedly close friends. Come to find out they were not my friends at all. I found out that the very one's I called my friends and confided in were the very people telling anyone they could. They were the main ones talking about me.

I was so grateful for my mom during my pregnancy. She helped me through it. I couldn't have made it without her. I was so upset with myself, but she was so calm with me. Her calm and caring spirit helped me come back to myself. I really didn't know how to wrap my head around the fact that I was going to have a baby. I was a baby having a baby.

My delivery date was fast approaching. I had so many emotions going on all at one time. I was worried about how labor and delivery was going to go. I did not know what to expect. I had not talked to Leonardo. I was so distracted. When I went into labor he did not know.

Before the labor, I was trying to prepare myself. I had my bag packed so when I went into labor I would be ready. Of course it didn't happen like it was supposed to. I got to the hospital. They put me in a room. I was in labor for hours. It hurt like hell! The next thing I knew, they were prepping me for an emergency c-section. OMG!

The next thing I knew I heard a baby crying. They told me it was a girl. They cleaned her and brought her to me. She was beautiful.

I got back to the room and I do not know who told Leonardo but he was there. He was intoxicated. He said he was happy we had a baby girl and she was healthy. I was overwhelmed with emotion. I was just trying to adjust to everything that was going on at that moment.

Despite me having a c-section, they did not keep me in the hospital long. In a couple of days, we were home and bonding. It did take some getting used to getting up every four hours to feed and change her diapers. After a while, I got used to it.

When my six weeks of recovery were up I had to go back to school and face my schoolmates. It wasn't an easy transition for me. I was embarrassed and ashamed, and I had to face all the questions and people passing judgment on me. I was not prepared for the wrath I went through going back to school. I had to endure being talked about and all the whispering. It was very overwhelming.

Baby Daddy Drama

Despite all of that, after our daughter was born, Leonardo was around off and on. It caused me so many mental and emotional changes. We were both so young and so much in love, but now I had a life I was responsible for. I was responsible for a life, but I had no control in or over my own life. It was for sure an emotional roller coaster.

Here I was just after turning fifteen and I was someone's mom. I was really trying to learn how to be one. However, I still needed guidance and direction myself. I wasn't sure whether I could do it or not. Every day was a challenge. Some days, it was overwhelming. I often felt like giving up. Something had to give. I just wanted something to go right. I had made so many mistakes already.

Leonardo wasn't ready at all! He was still a hormonal teenager. He was confused and not sure of what direction he wanted to go in. We were together off and on four years after our daughter was born. During that time, he talked to me about wanting to go into the air force. I wasn't happy about that at all. I felt like he should stay and help me take care of our daughter. Despite how I felt, he decided to do it. I suppose he thought it would give him some kind of career and help him mature somehow.

While he was in boot camp, he was writing me letters. He would tell me how hard it was. He kept telling me how much he loved and missed me and our daughter. He said he wanted us to be a family. I thought it was just loneliness and home sickness talking. He had been in boot camp about six weeks. I don't know what happened. I never really got the full details. Next thing I knew, he was writing to tell me he would be coming home.

He came home with an honorable discharge. We never really talked about it much. When he got back home, he would come over to spend time and help me with the baby. I was thinking maybe there was some hope for us after all. I guess all this family bonding we were doing made him say the next words that came out of his mouth. He talked to me about us being a family. He wanted to get married.

I wasn't sure if I was ready for that. I still wanted to try. I wanted to give it a chance. Maybe, somehow, I could make my wrong a right! I said yes. A few months later, we got married. My parents weren't happy at all! They thought we were too young.

When my wedding day came around, I was getting a little apprehensive myself. I was so nervous. I guess it was cold feet. Maybe it was a sign I ignored. I felt weird about it the entire time before the ceremony, but I went through with it anyway.

We had the wedding at the church we attended. I was over an hour late for the ceremony. What a disaster! But even with all that, I felt it was what I should do. I felt like I was somewhat grown up after having a baby and I needed to be on my own. Making my own rules. You know how young people think sometimes. We just want to get out of our parent's house and on our own. Too many rules. If I knew then, what I know now, I would have listened to them. We were so-called grown kids thinking we knew everything. We did not realize we still needed structure and discipline.

So there I was. Nineteen and trying to be a wife and a mother. I was struggling with both. I had not yet fully grasped being a mother, now I was a wife. You ever heard the saying "you can't see the forest for the trees"? That was a very true statement in my case. I think sometimes as young adults we feel that we have more answers than our parents do. We feel like all they do is yell and tell us what to do. It causes us to rebel. Making our relationships with our parents not so good.

But I understand my parent's disappointment. I became a wife and a mother at a young age. I am sure that wasn't their expectations for me. It wasn't mine either. I battled with myself constantly. Wondering whether I was good enough after the shameful and embarrassing things I felt I had done in my life.

Not long after the wedding, things really changed. The guy I was so involved with, that I have a beautiful child with and have now married began abusing me. He abused me routinely, both physically and mentally. I was devastated and even more ashamed. I didn't ask to be treated like this. I didn't do anything to deserve it either. I was so unsure of myself. I had no clue how to fix myself or this situation. Another situation I could not fix.

I wanted my mom and dad to be proud of me. I wanted to prove to them, after I got married, that I could hold it down and make it work. But another dream was crumbling. I was so broken. My heart needed healing and so did my soul.

I tried to hold my head up, but on the inside, my heart was breaking. There was nothing harder than trying to keep it together. In spite of my efforts, it was really coming unraveled. My faith had really wavered. I knew God was there. He always was, but I was wallowing in my own stuff. I wasn't listening to him. Truth is, I couldn't hear or understand him. I could not see my way, even though I really needed God. I would pray and ask for God's help, but I really don't think I was ready to receive it at that time. I was under some serious spiritual warfare and trying to fight my way back. I was totally disgusted with myself.

CHAPTER THREE

Journey Like No Other

So you know how it is, going from living with your parents to living with your husband. I tried to do the best that I could. Little did I know what I had gotten myself into. I would try to be the best young wife I could be. I tried to treat him like I would want to be treated. That was all I knew to do. We started out trying to find our way. It was so much to handle because we were going into this marriage blind with a new baby.

We thought we were in love and that that was enough. Despite us having so much to learn, I was going to do my best to make it work. However, we apparently had different thoughts on what marriage was about. He was starting to be a little controlling. I thought marriage was supposed to be a partnership. In the complex we lived in at the time, there were some married couples and singles. I would talk to my neighbors some times in passing. Whether they were married or single, my communication with the neighbors disturbed Leonardo. I guess in his head he thought it was more than that with some of the male neighbors, but it was not true.

He started accusing me of talking to them intimately. As if, it was taking all the energy had to deal with one, so that wasn't going on at all. He also started saying really nasty things to me. When I would dress up to go out somewhere. I thought I looked nice. He would tell me how unattractive I was. He would say, "Who would want to look at you?" It quickly became frustrating! I didn't understand where these things were coming from. Something was not quite right, things were changing with him fast.

My feelings soon proved true. I found out later some of the people he was calling his friends were the wrong crowd of people to be around. He would come home from being with those particular friends and he would act differently and pick fights with me. I wasn't sure if he was drinking or doing drugs or both. I sensed something wasn't right. I knew whatever it was he was doing, it turned him into a whole different person!

I figured out over some period of time he was using drugs. It was difficult after discovering that he was using. His mood swings! His short temper! I decided to send our daughter to her grandmother's, my mom, for a while. I wanted her to be safe. It was one thing for me to go through it, but I did not want this for her. I did not want her to know what was going on at all. That was the decision I made. I would just have to go home to my mom's and visit her until things calmed down. It was no place for a child.

I was praying he would get a grip on himself. He was totally treating me like crap. He would apologize and tell me he loved me and that he would do better. He sounded so sincere when he apologized. I loved him, and I wanted to give him another chance. It got very frustrating because he would only do well for a short time. Then he would go right back to his old ways. At this point, we started fighting all the time. Here I was a newlywed, and everything was going to hell in a hand basket already! I definitely had no honeymoon stage. I felt like such a loser. I was just starting out and my marriage was already a mess. I regretted being in the marriage. What was I supposed to do now?

I would hear over and over in my head the words of the older church mothers that I looked to for guidance whenever I would want to leave. They would say, "Baby, you have to stay and work out your marriage." I think they forgot to tell me about all the emotional things I would go through and how it would affects me long term by staying.

Oh my goodness, it wasn't easy at all. I guess I tried to fake it until I could make it. I realized that I had bitten off more than I could chew. But. This was my bed and I had to lie in it. I guess, even though I thought and say I loved him, I had no idea what that was.

I thought the drama was just a rough spot in my marriage. Thank God for my parents. I would not have made it without their guidance. I also would not have been married at nineteen if I had listened to them before. Why didn't I listen!

As you get older, you realize everything your parents told you would happen ends up happening. I guess being young we think our parents are lame and so not cool. I found out that was not true. They loved me and they only had my best interest at heart. And they have seen and experienced a lot in life.

I wish I could have thrown in the towel and gone back home, and started over. I didn't because I thought I would hear, "I told you so," and all that stuff. That was not what I wanted or needed to hear. I needed something to work out for me. I just tried to stick it out, but what a bumpy ass ride!

CHAPTER FOUR

Faith of a Mustard Seed

I was always on my knees praying for God's help and favor. You know the lines to the gospel song: "He may not come when you want him, but he'll be there right on time!" I had been through so much physical and mental abuse. I didn't know how much more I could take. I had lost sight of myself totally. I felt like I was at the end of my rope. A friend of mine invited Leonardo and I to church during their revival. Once we entered the service, it was as if God was speaking to both of us. That night in the service changed our lives.

After the revival was over, we started going back to church on a regular basis again. What a blessing! Things were starting to look up. Not long after that, Leonardo came to me and said God had called him to preach. He went to the pastor and asked if he could preach sometime. He was actually doing pretty well at it, so he decided to try him out. He began preaching on a regular basis. Things started going well again at home. That was a nice welcoming change.

The Romance Is Back

Leonardo started romancing me again. He made me remember why I fell in love with him in the first place. I started feeling like I could be happy again. We started going on weekend trips. We went out to romantic dinners and just really enjoyed each other.

He even surprised me one time for our anniversary and took me to this beautiful cabin style hotel. It was like a honeymoon. We didn't get a chance to have one when we got married. But it felt like we were having one now. It was wonderful! I was praying with all my heart that it would last. I wanted our marriage to work.

Unfortunately, the streak didn't last. I noticed the old friends had started creeping back around. I guess he wasn't strong enough to fight it like he thought.

OH MY GOODNESS! The next six or seven years were pure hell! I tried to stay and work through it, like the older church mothers had said. It wasn't easy at all. With all the arguments and the fights, it was worse than ever before. I didn't know what things would set him off, so I really tried to be careful of my actions. He would get upset and go off on me for no reason.

One time while he was talking to me, he caught me off guard and hit me square in my face. He hit me so hard he dislocated my jaw. I wasn't able to go to the doctor at the time because we had no insurance. To this day, it bothers me. I have lived with it all this time.

I could not even begin to know how to explain what happened during that conversation or why he did it. I stop asking him why.

When it came to sexual relations in our marriage, I would have to fight him off. He was forcing himself on me. I don't know how, after all the abuse I had been through with him, he would think I would want to be bothered at all. He forced himself on me regularly and got to the point where he would sodomize me repeatedly by force. He was always accusing me of fooling around on him. Justifying his actions. I was so stressed out and confused. I did not know what to do. I couldn't tell anyone.

I was worried about someone finding out what I was really going through. I was so ashamed and worried that somebody would tell me how stupid I was for putting up with all of this. I know people always say, you could have found someone to talk to. "Yeah, right," I had tried that before many times before and it never worked out well for me. I felt that whoever I talked to would only judge me anyway. I beat up on myself so much. I felt like I let my parents down, my daughter as well as myself.

Really Bad Timing

After all I had been through, I found out I was pregnant with our second child. It wasn't a happy pregnancy like it should have been. I was stressed out and crying all the time. I didn't take care of myself at all. He would start with that same crap, accusing me of fooling around on him. "Really? Really!"

I was pregnant. I was working all the time, and he was not working at the time at all. As a matter of fact, I was working two jobs while I was pregnant. He was home all day, and he did not help me with cleaning or anything. He would leave it for me to do when I got off.

Even though he was treating me like shit, I tried not to break his spirit when he was not working and could not find a job. I only wish he would have known how to return the favor. I would work until late at night. I was exhausted.

The controlling went from one extreme to the other. He wanted me to clean and then he didn't want me to clean. If I didn't clean he would use it to pick a fight with me the next morning.

We were arguing one time and instead of us both getting heated, I decided to leave so we could cool off. As I am walking down the stairs to leave, he decided to pick up the television and throw it down the stairs at me. It hit me and grazed across my back.

I was pregnant at the time. I truly was going through some kind of hell. I know you are probably wondering why I was still hanging in there. But like most young girls who have never experienced any other guy, this was my first love. He was my high school sweetheart. He was my first everything.

He began begging me to forgive him and telling me he loved me. He just didn't want me to leave him. He asked me to give him yet again, another chance to get it right.

I don't know if my hormones were wreaking havoc on my emotions, but I gave him yet another chance. I was on such an emotional roller coaster. At the same time if forgave him, I was so disappointed in myself. I was pregnant again in this messed up union I was in and did not know how to get out. I had so many thoughts going through my mind, and none of them were good.

I was pregnant, emotionally all over the place, not eating well at all. I had no proper health care at the time either. My spirit was so low down. I just kept pushing myself despite being an emotional wreck.

When I was working, I worked in a kitchen. I would have to pick up heavy trays full of dishes to put in the dishwasher. This one night at work, I went to pick up a tray of dishes and I got a very bad pain in my stomach. It was so bad I had to go to the emergency room. I went into early labor, and I had to stay at the hospital until the contractions stopped. There was so much turmoil going on, I was just trying to make it through it all. But it was getting to me.

CHAPTER FIVE

Didn't See This Coming

I would have never thought in a million years my day would end up with me getting shot. Leonardo came in the house from work. I don't know if he had had a bad day or what, but he walked into the house with an attitude and started an argument with me for no reason once again. During the time of this argument, I was in the kitchen cleaning up. We exchanged some harsh words. We were arguing to the point he ended up all in my face. I was very scared. I had to pick up a knife and shake it at him to get him away from me. I wasn't sure what he would do because of the things I had experienced with him in the past. He walked away. After that I put the knife back in the sink.

I decided to leave so it wouldn't escalate any further. I went to the closet to put my coat on before leaving. He called out to me, only for me to look at him pointing a gun at me from the bedroom. I was in shock, and I just froze. I asked him what he was doing. He didn't respond to that question. Pow! I was shot!

If he had not called my name before he shot I would not have moved my head, which was in front of my hand holding the closet door. The bullet would have gone right through my temple. Instead, when he fired the gun, the bullet hit me in the hand which was still holding the door. The bullet went in and didn't come out.

I couldn't move. I was in such shock. I couldn't believe my husband had shot me! I could not believe it had gotten this far. There was so much blood. It looked like the scene of a horror movie gone bad. I think after the smoke cleared, he saw me holding my hand and all the blood that was squirting out of my hand and realized what he did. He was terrified.

Headed to the Hospital

I had never seen so much blood. It was squirting out like a water fountain. Leonardo wrapped my hand up and put me in the car. The whole ride to the hospital, he was apologizing and telling me how much he loved me. Yes, again.

It really got to him seeing all the blood. He was so nervous. I would have thought it would be me freaked out and panicky, but amazingly, I was pretty calm. I'm sure my body was in shock mode, and that was why. It was unbelievable that something like this could have happened. It is not something you think of happening to you. It is a line you don't think will ever be crossed.

Once I entered the emergency room, things began moving so fast. They took me right in for emergency surgery. They told me it was a possibility that I could lose my middle finger on my right hand. They were worried. They did not know if they could save it or not. I was in surgery for eight hours. I am so grateful to God for working through the surgeons. They were able to save my finger. *Glory is to God!!*

Jail Time

I found out after coming out of surgery that the police had talked to Leonardo and he had told them what had happened. They immediately arrested him. He was in jail for a week. I was in the hospital for a week recovering. When he did get out, he came straight home. He told me how sorry he was, like he had done so many times before, and he wanted our marriage to work. Do you know, after everything that happened, they gave him back his gun and didn't give me back my kitchen knife! What kind of shit is that? It made no sense to me at all. But it sent a clear message.

I know you are still wondering what the hell I was thinking. I had so many things going through my head. I was thinking I believed that I loved him so much that I could help change him. I also knew when he wasn't doing drugs, he was that person I had fallen in love with. I thought all these things at the time would be enough to save him. I had so many physical and emotional issues myself. I didn't know what was real and what wasn't.! I wanted to make it work. I wanted to prove to myself that I wasn't a total failure. I didn't say I was thinking clearly or that I always made the right decisions.

I guess I felt at the time it was my cross to bear. When someone you love tells you he is sorry, you want to forgive and believe them. How does that saying go?

Insanity is when you keep doing the same thing over expecting different results! "INSANITY"! I guess my problem was I always hoped for the best. I hoped someday it would change.

CHAPTER SIX

The Fallout

L eonardo and I had been home together for a
while after this ordeal. It was very
interesting. I know by now you think I had
lost my damn mind. What in God's name was I
doing?!!! I understand that you can totally do some
things that make no sense until you find your way. I
either had temporarily lost my mind or I had the most
forgiving heart despite what I've been through.

After being home with me for a while, Leonardo's
mind was getting the best of him. It got so bad he even
started accusing me of poisoning his food. I wasn't. His
conscience was killing him. It wasn't even a thought on
my part, but he didn't trust me. Go figure! I think it
should have been the other way around

For me, I just wanted to forgive him from my heart
and try to make it work. I felt that way even though he
claimed he was uneasy around me. Yet, he still
continued to do annoying crap to me.

Back at Work

I finally recovered. I was able to go back to
work. I was working next door to where we lived at
the time. One day I went to work like I did the same
time every day. I forgot something at home that I
needed. I went home on my break to get it, only to find
a woman in my house with my husband. He told me to

just get what I needed, not to say anything, and go back
to work. I did! My first thought was, *"how stupid can I
be?"* My next thought was to kick my husband's ass
after all the nonsense I had been through with him.

I know that wouldn't have gone well because I
couldn't win. I told myself I was working and there was
nothing I could do about it at the moment. It was the
longest night ever. I was so frustrated. I decided to try
to call him on my next break. Would you believe the
woman who was there earlier answered the phone? I
couldn't get over it! What the hell had I gotten into?
Really!

I worked my shift until it was over and dealt with it
when I got home. He was very smug about it. I felt
betrayed and hurt. I had no idea what to do. My self-
esteem was at an all-time low. I had no one to talk to.
No one I could trust. I was worried if I told somebody
about what was going on, he or she would tell me how
stupid I was. I felt like such a disappointment and
failure to my own self.

CHAPTER SEVEN
Living with My Demons

With all the things I had been through, I wondered why I couldn't get it together. Why was I trying so hard to make it work? I had so many thoughts going on in my head. I felt like I wasn't good enough or that I didn't deserve to be loved. I had two daughters,' Tiffani and Tamyka, and I was trying to be a good mom to them. I was trying to do the best I could and stay a family. My self-esteem was literally on the bottom of my shoe. I could not see a way beyond where I was. What was I teaching my babies? I never wanted my girls to go through the things I had been through in my life. But this, was no life.

Everyone needs someone they can confide in some time or another. I thought I had found that friend I could talk to. I decided to open up and put myself out there.

Just when I thought I could trust someone again, she turned on me. That so-called friend ended up telling other people all my personal business. Here I was again. I was so devastated.

People were talking about me behind my back and smiling in my face. I was trying so hard to work through my feelings. Do you know how hard it is to open up to anyone when someone has already betrayed you with your deepest darkest secrets and shames? It caused me to shut up and shut down.

Facing My Own Demons

I just wanted to bury everything deep down inside. I kept it all in. It made me distance myself from people period! Damn, people can be so cruel, thoughtless, and totally unfeeling until it's all about them. I was damaged from the physical and sexual abuse. I didn't know whom I could talk to or whom I could trust.

Sometimes people treat you any way they want without any regard for the fallout that occurs from their actions. I didn't want anyone to go through the hurt and pain like I had. I worried constantly about what people thought about me. An added burden on top of everything else. Some people are just something else. Instead of lifting you up, they make it their mission to tear you down. I had never done anything to any of them, but they decided they didn't like me and therefore it was okay to cause me pain and anguish in my time of despair. I never understood how people could bad mouth you when they didn't even know you.

Most people take your kindness for weakness. Then they wonder why you are stand offish. They mistake being quiet for being antisocial. I am so glad I still have a forgiving heart after all the shenanigans I've been through. I have room to love people and not react to them like they did to me when really I shouldn't have given any of them a pass at all.

You know, sometimes the things you go through in your life can cause you to make some very bad decisions. I had regrets about some of them. It wasn't easy. I was so disappointed. Especially in myself. When it came to men, it was beyond my understanding. I never seemed to pick the right one. I was looking for someone to love me and tell me I was the one- as all young ladies do. I didn't realize so many were full of a bunch of crap and they just tell you what you want to hear so they can sleep with you! Go figure. It took me a while to understand that you should not take someone at his or her word. It was so bad, I got to the point I trusted no one.

I didn't want to get dressed or get out of bed. I had been through a million changes and back! I went from being angry to crying to feeling betrayed and used. I had a plethora of changes going on. I promised myself no matter how crappy people had treated me in the past, my heart wouldn't allow me to stoop to the same level as they had. I know what it is like to be hurt and let down. It is the worst.

I found some inner strength to know I wanted to give my family and my few good friends the love I never got. I did learn how to be a good friend and love my family members unconditionally. I know people can say and do hurtful things to you that can affect your whole life!

I lived by the fake- it- till- I- could- make- it motto. I do revert back to that when I need too. It is a lonely place to be. Dealing with so much and having no one to trust to unload the burden was devastating. I was so stressed out. It takes so much energy to keep things under wraps.

Leonardo was a preacher at this time, but not treating me well at all. Definitely not like a preacher should. However, I did not want to talk to the pastor. I didn't want to talk to any therapist either because I figured I would be a case study and he or she really couldn't or wouldn't help me at all.

As much as I disliked the thought, I knew I still needed to speak to a professional. I thought maybe a therapist could at least help me sort out some of these stressful emotions I was going through. The opportunity arouse for me to be able to talk to a counselor.

I was very nervous about going to this appointment because it meant I had to open up. That wasn't easy for me. I had had a big wall up for so long after so many let downs. Once we started, I did open up and talk some. I didn't open up all the way because of past experiences with people violating my trust. I have to admit that I did feel somewhat better after the conversation. But, it made me feel so vulnerable. I went that one time only to see a counselor and have never been back since. I gave it a chance. In the end, I supposed that with time the heartache would repair itself and I would come out somewhat whole and victorious. That was my hope.

CHAPTER EIGHT

End of My Rope

I finally, at some point, realized enough was enough. I had given it all I could, and I had no more to give. I finally got up the nerve to leave Leonardo. It truly was a struggle for me to do it. I didn't look back, like I had so many times before. I finally left Decatur. My babies and I moved back to Joliet. I started over and began picking up the pieces of my damn screwed- up life.

I had no idea where to begin. I was broken, and I surely needed to be fixed. I had to figure out how to start loving myself again. My way of dealing with it at the time was staying in the house. I would stay away from people as much as I could. I had to force myself to get out of the bed. I had to make myself get dressed too. I would use that fake-it- till- I- could- make- it policy. Good luck with that! It was a long and painful journey for me.

My Struggle

I listened to some people tell me I had a pretty face but I needed to lose some weight. Such a horrible backhanded comment. I was nice enough not to mention their flaws and issues. I truly knew firsthand how it felt for someone to insult you to your face. So I refrained from giving them the same disrespect in return. I mean really, do you think people who are overweight don't know that already? They do every day of their lives. They don't need anyone else to bring that to their attention.

You don't know what people are going through so it is best to shut up! You can be healthy, exercise and still be overweight in other people's eyes. You can have a medical condition, or have been sexually molested and gain weight as a result of the non-comfortability in your own skin. If you don't know what that person has been through, you really can't speak on it, nor should you speak on them. They have had enough of that already.

Here I was attempting to put back the pieces of an unrealized life and I had no one I could trust or talk to at about any of it. Food became my go to comfort! The first reason is, food doesn't talk back. It doesn't put you down. It doesn't judge you or call you names. It doesn't talk about you behind your back. It gives you whatever you want from it. It pleases you and meets your need.

I knew I had to change my thinking process though. I was much more comfortable with eating food than interacting with people. This was not what I wanted. It was not the normal I desired. I had to figure a way out.

It was a task to start to learn about myself again. I wasn't sure if I knew myself at all, but I had to figure it out. I had to start somewhere. I decided to start to analyze the food I was consuming and start to change that. That was something I could change. It was a tangible thing I could control. So I started where I had control. I cut out some thing's, began eating healthier, and doing some exercise. I had to talk to my self regularly to stay on track.

I tried to work on the outside first, hoping it would help the broken inside at some point. I had to learn how to love and care about myself. I had to understand that I was worth it and not worthless. I had to realize I mattered in this world. It was a true struggle.

It was so easy to want to go back to old habits because when you're on your weight loss journey you have to be your own cheerleader. No one really wants you to succeed. They like you right where you are. That way they can define you against themselves. I realized I had to continually find the strength inside myself if I was going to achieve my goals. I wanted so much more for my girls. I wanted be a better mother. A better woman for my girls. I would always tell them they could do anything they put their minds too. I wanted to show them as well.

I would let them know how beautiful and smart they were. I never wanted them to go through the things I had been through- ever. I wanted to be the best mom that I could. I wanted to protect them in everything. Even though I knew in my heart it wasn't possible, but I damn sure was going to try. I didn't want to be such a letdown to them. I wanted them to be proud of me.

Motherhood didn't come with a manual, so you learned by trial and error. Balancing everything is overwhelming at times. Sometimes, trying to do the logical and expected things, like keeping bills paid and a roof over our heads, I hated. It meant I had to sacrifice the time I could spend with my girls to provide the basic necessities. But that is part of motherhood, huh.

What I had to realize and get through to myself was that it didn't matter what anyone else thought about me. I had to have confidence in myself and do the best I could. I would walk in rooms or upon people having conversations and realize they were talking about me. Calling me lazy, unhealthy, and whatever else. It was so not true. I was working my butt off and carrying my own heavy load of life. It reinforced my internalizing and self-cheerleading. I hadn't gotten to the place yet to realize I wasn't the problem. It was not until later that I understood that the ones who were talking about me, had to find flaws in me so they wouldn't have to concentrate on their own issues. Sooner or later, I found out they all had them.

Despite all efforts to move ahead, I was in need of some healing. I equated being silent with being strong. It only causes you to bury things even deeper.

Then, something happened one day. It was like a trigger. A memory came up and out. And then I thought, "to get where you need to be, you have to remember where you've been. It's how you deal with your issues and come out of it that counts!" I had to figure out how to turn my fear into confidence.

I was for sure gun shy after the things I had been through in my life. I was very cautious and apprehensive around people. I had been stabbed in the back so many times there was nowhere else to stick me. So I tested the waters with different people. I would tell them some half truths about myself to see what would happen. It was hard for me to trust so I had to get past this impasse. Sure enough, failure upon failure. When the smoke settled and the information got back to me, there would be so much more added to the story, and of course, none of it was true.

I got tired of putting my heart on the line and getting it massacred. It was hard to recovery from that with each and every disappointment. I still kept putting my heart out there though. Trying to have a real, truthful and trusting relationship with someone. It couldn't get any worse. The only way I could go was up. That was my hope anyway!

CHAPTER NINE

Starting Over

Starting over was a constant struggle. I knew somewhere deep in my heart I was worth it though. I still wasn't totally convinced despite years passing, but I was moving. Though I was moving, the weight of yesterday never seemed to let up. It was almost haunting.

I had been away from Leonardo about eleven years now. We were still legally married, just not living together anymore. I decided it was finally time to start the process of getting a divorce and give the relationship closure. While I was starting this process, I received a phone call that Leonardo had gotten married again!

I guess because so much time had gone by, he thought we weren't still married. I told them, "Surprise!" We are still legally in a union."LOL"! I didn't make a big deal about it. I was so glad to be away from him. I had someone in the family let him know that his new wife wasn't legitimate. Then, I moved forward with the divorce. I was so glad when it was final. It was like I could breathe again! It was a long process though. Divorce is never good; it's the breakdown of something that was supposed to last forever. Despite the relief, I was still on an emotional rollercoaster. It was like I lost a piece of myself. You feel like you can never get that piece of yourself back again!

My divorce was finally done and over with. I was relieved as well as scared. There was no more hope for that being anything other than what was. Now, it was truly about me and my babies. I had to try to go on with my life and get back on my feet knowing for sure, it was all on me. I was now officially a single mom.

I had one more thing to feel inadequate about. It was now just the girls and I. I had to try my best to see the light at the end of the tunnel. While at the same time working on myself. I was overwhelmed by it all at first. It came with a lot of tears and setbacks. I had to push my way through to encourage myself and try to keep my head up. I had to live as normally as I could for the girls so it wouldn't affect them.

There were a number of rough days. I didn't want them to see me cry. I would wake up some mornings and wouldn't feel like getting out of bed, but I had to push my way through for my girls. I had to try to give them a decent life. I truly had to work on building my faith. I did eventually get stronger on my feet as I prayed constantly on my knees.

Praise God, things started to turn around. I did get a job and was better able to take care of the girls. What a blessing that was! It was a start for sure. I had to play catchup with everything. But, I was grateful to be able to finally do that. Even though I finally had a job, it wasn't paying much money. I had to make due during this time. I was always looking for a better job and something with health benefits for the girls. They were having some asthma and ear infection issues. I stayed at the emergency room with them, which racked up a lot of bills. I did what I had to do. Along with the full-time job, I had two part-time jobs working thirty-five additional hours a piece per week just to make ends meet.

Unreal! Unbelievable!

I was living my life on my own terms when I got a call that would change my whole understanding. In June 2005, I got a call that Leonardo Drisdel had brutally killed Cassandra Kovac. I was in absolute shock! I realized for sure at that moment he had issues much deeper than I did or that I could have loved him through. I had acquired some issues from being with him without a doubt! But I could not have fixed him, no matter how hard I tried. I immediately hung up from the call with tears running down my face. Thanking God and being grateful, because that could have very well been me. The help he needed was nothing I could have given to him.

I realized that everything that happened to me wasn't my fault. All the lies said about me and all the things done to me were not true and were not my fault. I really thought my love for him would save him or at least be reciprocated. When I let that idea go, I really ended up finally saving myself. My God, so many things were going through my head. I replayed all the things he had done to me over and over again. I just thought to myself at any time the things that happened could have ended up with me just like her. I might not have been around at all. So much was lifted from me. Such clarity came to me in the midst of the sadness of this news. I thank God for his favor, grace, and mercy. I hold on to the thought that God protected me and "that God doesn't put on us more than we can bear" I am strong. I am worthy. My journey, by far, is not yet over!

***

GLOSSARY OF TERMS

Awkward	Clumsy
LOL	Laugh Out Loud
Complicated	To make or become more complex
Hormones	A product of living cells
Virginity	One who never engaged in sexual activity
Transition	Instance of changing from one to another state
Revert	To return to and earlier state
Devastated	To overwhelm
Flaws	An imperfect blemish
BBW	Big beautiful woman
Molested	To accost sexually
Afflictions	To inflict physical or mental suffering on
Naive	Lacking sophistication and worldly experience
Innocent	Free from sin and wrong doing
Husky	Strong and ruggedly built
Panicky	A sudden overpowering fear
Internalize	To make internal, personal or subjective
Logical	Reasonable
Sodomize	A form of sexual intercourse held to be unnatural or abnormal example: anal copulation

www.ingramcontent.com/pod-product-compliance
Lightning Source LLC
Chambersburg PA
CBHW060202070426

42447CB00033B/2307